A Three-Hour Service For Good Friday

Reflections From The Cross

William Dexter Moser, Jr.

CSS Publishing Company, Inc., Lima, Ohio

A THREE-HOUR SERVICE FOR GOOD FRIDAY

Copyright © 1997 by
CSS Publishing Company, Inc.
Lima, Ohio

The original purchaser may photocopy material in this publication for use as it was intended (i.e. worship material for worship use; educational material for classroom use; dramatic material for staging or production). No additional permission is required from the publisher for such copying by the original purchaser only. Inquiries should be addressed to: Permissions, CSS Publishing Company, Inc., P.O. Box 4503, Lima, Ohio 45802-4503.

Scripture quotations are from the *New Revised Standard Version of the Bible*, copyright 1989 by the Division of Christian Education of the National Council of the Churches of Christ in the USA. Used by permission.

Library of Congress Cataloging-in-Publication Data

Moser, William D., 1918-
   A three-hour service for Good Friday / William D. Moser
     p.   cm.
   ISBN 0-7880-1136-7 (pbk.)
     1. Good Friday—Liturgies—Texts. 2. Good Friday—Meditations. I. Title.
BV95.M66   1998
264—dc21   97-29590
                                                                                 CIP

ISBN 0-7880-1136-7   PRINTED IN U.S.A.

In honor of my wife
Elizabeth Cobb Moser

Foreword

In preparing *A Three-Hour Service For Good Friday,* The Reverend William Dexter Moser has rendered a great service to the worshiping community. He has skillfully captured the power and the pathos of the most sacred day in the life of the Church in the fundamental beginning of hymn, confession, creed, and prayers. The service leads the worshiper through the grief and the glory of the Crucifixion. The original poetry of Rev. Moser adds personal conviction and emotional power to the deep reflective mood of the three-hour vigil. This service can be used in any worship context by those who wish once more to stand in loving sorrow at the foot of the cross.

Dr. Robert F. Sims, Senior Pastor
Lutheran Church of the Redeemer
Atlanta, Georgia

Introduction

The three-hour Good Friday worship services which I have experienced over the years of my life have been most inspirational to me in my childhood, my youth, and my adult years.

The Lenten and the Holy Week services have been very meaningful spiritual experiences. The various worship opportunities in a variety of church facilities have been offered in many quiet, dignified, beautiful surroundings. Each of these has given the best of skilled artists in the field of church professionals and dedicated volunteers.

It has been my gift of life to have Christian parents and thus be offered a church life that led me through childhood to adulthood in the richness of the Christian experience.

It has been a joy of my life to attempt to express some of my feelings and thoughts of this Christian life through the writing of poetry. It has been most gratifying to me to be able to write and incorporate some of that poetry in this service. It is my fervent prayer that this service of worship will be spiritually meaningful to each of you who worship in and through this printed service in your own congregation.

May the blessings of Christ continue to enrich each of us as we serve in his great and glorious kingdom!

William Dexter Moser, Jr.

A Three-Hour Service For Good Friday

Reflections From The Cross

12:00 Noon to 3:00 P.M.

(Congregation stands for hymns.)

Hymn   "O Master, Let Me Walk With You"
O Master, let me walk with you
In lowly paths of service true;
Tell me your secret; help me bear
The strain of toil, the fret of care.

Help me the slow of heart to move
By some clear, winning word of love;
Teach me the wayward feet to stay,
And guide them in the homeward way.

Teach me your patience; share with me
A closer, dearer company,
In work that keeps faith sweet and strong,
In trust that triumphs over wrong,

In hope that sends a shining ray
Far down the future's broadening way,
In peace that only you can give;
With you, O Master, let me live.
                (Washington Gladden, 1836-1918)

Minister: The grace of our Lord Jesus Christ, the love of God, and the fellowship of the Holy Spirit be with you all.

People: **Amen.**

Psalm 51

Minister: Have mercy on me, O God,
according to your steadfast love;
according to your abundant mercy
blot out my transgressions.

People: **Wash me thoroughly from my iniquity,
and cleanse me from my sin.**

Minister: For I know my transgressions,
and my sin is ever before me.

People: **Against you, you alone, have I sinned,
and done what is evil in your sight,
so that you are justified in your sentence
and blameless when you pass judgment.**

Minister: Indeed, I was born guilty,
a sinner when my mother conceived me.

People: **You desire truth in the inward being;
therefore teach me wisdom in
my secret heart.**

Minister: Purge me with hyssop, and I shall be clean;
wash me, and I shall be whiter than snow.

People: **Let me hear joy and gladness;
let the bones that you have crushed rejoice.**

Minister: Hide your face from my sins,
and blot out my iniquities.

People: **Create in me a clean heart, O God,
and put a new and right spirit within me.**

Minister: Do not cast me away from your presence,
and do not take your holy spirit from me.

People: **Restore to me the joy of your salvation,
and sustain in me a willing spirit.**

Minister: Then I will teach transgressors your ways,
and sinners will return to you.

People: **Deliver me from bloodshed, O God,
O God of my salvation,
and my tongue will sing aloud
of your deliverance.**

Minister: O Lord, open my lips,
and my mouth will declare your praise.

People: **For you have no delight in sacrifice;
if I were to give a burnt offering,
you would not be pleased.**

Minister: The sacrifice acceptable to God
is a broken spirit;
a broken and contrite heart, O God,
you will not despise.

People: **Do good to Zion in your good pleasure;
rebuild the walls of Jerusalem.**

A Statement of Christian Belief
(From portions of the Athanasian Creed)
All: **"... We worship one God in Trinity and the Trinity
in unity, neither confusing the persons nor dividing
the divine being, for the Father is one person, the
Son is another, and the Spirit is still another.**

But the deity of the Father, Son, and Holy Spirit is one, equal in glory, co-eternal in majesty. What the Father is, the Son is, and so is the Holy Spirit. Uncreated is the Father, uncreated is the Son, uncreated is the Spirit. The Father is infinite, the Son is infinite, the Holy Spirit is infinite.

Eternal is the Father, eternal is the Son, eternal is the Spirit ... whoever wants to be saved should think thus about the Trinity. It is necessary for eternal salvation that one also faithfully believes that our Lord Jesus Christ became flesh.

For this is true faith that we believe and confess: That our Lord Jesus Christ, God's Son, is both God and man ... He suffered death for our salvation ... He rose again from the dead. He ascended into heaven and is seated at the right hand of the Father. He will come again to judge the living and the dead ... One cannot be saved without believing this firmly and faithfully."

The Prayer

Minister: To him who loves us and freed us from our sins with his life's blood, who made of us a royal house, to serve as the priests of his God and Father — to him be glory and dominion for ever and ever.

People: Amen.

Minister: We lift our voices in prayer to you, O Christ.

People: **As we come together to worship on this Good Friday,**

Minister: Our lives have been fully enriched by your life-giving Word.

People: May we be touched by the Gospel writers' accounts of these words, his words, given to us in the scriptures,

Minister: The account of your life before, during, and after your crucifixion.

People: O Lord, it is your gift to us as we hear again the recorded events of your hours upon the cross, high upon the crest of Golgotha.

Minister: O Christ, may we experience the courage, the strength, the compassion, the spirituality, the forgiveness, and the tender love you gave to each of us from there upon your cross.

People: May we return to our daily lives and share your gracious gift of life to all the world.

Minister: In your name we pray with you, as you taught us to pray:

All: Our Father, who art in heaven,
    hallowed be thy name,
    thy kingdom come,
    thy will be done,
        on earth as it is in heaven.

Give us this day our daily bread;
and forgive us our trespasses,
    as we forgive those
        who trespass against us;
and lead us not into temptation,
    but deliver us from evil.

For thine is the kingdom,
    and the power, and the glory,
    forever and ever. Amen.

The First Word From The Cross
12:10 P.M.

Hymn "Beneath The Cross Of Jesus"

Beneath the cross of Jesus I long to take my stand;
The shadow of a mighty rock within a weary land,
A home within a wilderness, a rest upon the way,
From the burning of the noontide heat and the burdens of the day.

Upon the cross of Jesus, my eye at times can see
The very dying form of one who suffered there for me.
And from my contrite heart, with tears, two wonders I confess:
The wonder of his glorious love and my unworthiness.

I take, O cross, your shadow for my abiding place;
I ask no other sunshine than the sunshine of his face;
Content to let the world go by, to know no gain nor loss,
My sinful self my only shame, my glory all, the cross.
(Elizabeth C. Clephane, 1830-1869)

Psalm 12

Minister: Help, O Lord, for there is no longer anyone who is godly;
the faithful have disappeared from humankind.

People: **They utter lies to each other; with flattering lips and a double heart they speak.**

Minister: May the Lord cut off all flattering lips,
the tongue that makes great boasts,

People: **Those who say, "With our tongues we will prevail; our lips are our own — who is our Master?"**

Minister: "Because the poor are despoiled, because the needy groan, I will rise up," says the Lord;
"I will place them in the safety for which they long."

People: The promises of the Lord are promises that are pure, silver refined in a furnace on the ground, purified seven times.

Minister: You, O Lord, will protect us; you will guard us from this generation forever.

People: **On every side the wicked prowl, as vileness is exalted among humankind.**

The Lesson Luke 23:26-34
Minister: *As they led him away, they seized a man, Simon of Cyrene, who was coming from the country, and they laid the cross on him, and made him carry it behind Jesus. A great number of the people followed him, and among them were women who were beating their breasts and wailing for him. But Jesus turned to them and said, "Daughters of Jerusalem, do not weep for me, but weep for yourselves and for your children. For the days are surely coming when they will say, 'Blessed are the barren, and the wombs that never bore, and the breasts that never nursed.' Then they will begin to say to the mountains, 'Fall on us'; and to the hills, 'Cover us.' For if they do this when the wood is green, what will happen when it is dry?"*

Two others also, who were criminals, were led away to be put to death with him. When they came to the place that is called The Skull, they crucified Jesus there with the criminals, one on his right and one on his left. Then Jesus said, "Father, forgive them; for they do not know what they are doing." And they cast lots to divide his clothing.

Meditation on the First Word from the Cross
"Father, forgive them; for they do not know what they are doing."
— Luke 23:34

They dropped the cross down
In a hole in the ground.
He didn't resist or scream high and loud,
But calmly viewed the gathering crowd.

He viewed the people standing by,
As they watched, he made no outcry.
There were some friends so dear and true,
Also high priests, soldiers a few;

Romans doing their job as soldiers would do.
The protesting crowd felt Christ was through.
They wanted the sign changed.
The "King of the Jews" majestically remained!

Though his body most painful be,
He thought, felt, compassion for enemy,
His first of seven words spoken here
Were lifted lovingly, clearly in the air.

"Father, forgive them ..." plainly he said,
And many a heart did bow its head.
For, yes, they knew what they had done
To God's own great, kindly Son.

Now, his words announced to those below,
Age after age will feel its glow
Even though wrong is often committed,
By faith in Christ we, yes, we are remitted.

"Father, forgive them; for they do not know what they are doing."
(WDM)

Hymn   "Jesus, In Thy Dying Woes" Part I
Jesus, in thy dying woes,
Even while thy life-blood flows,
Craving pardon for thy foes:
Hear us, holy Jesus.

Savior, for our pardon sue
When our sins thy pangs renew,
For we know not what we do:
Hear us, holy Jesus.

O may we, who mercy need,
Be like thee in heart and deed,
When with wrong our spirits bleed:
Hear us, holy Jesus.

(Thomas Benson Pollock, 1836-1896)

Prayer

Minister: Let us pray. "Let it be known to you therefore, my brothers ... as said by Paul, that through this man forgiveness is proclaimed to you; by this Jesus everyone who believes is set free from all those sins from which you could not be freed by the law...." (Acts 13:38-39)

People: **Bless us, that our sins may be forgiven.**

Minister: O Lord, "He destined us for adoption as his children through Jesus Christ, according to the good pleasure of his will, to the praise of his glorious grace ... in him we have redemption through his blood, the forgiveness of our trespasses according to the riches of his grace." (Ephesians 13:5-7)

People: **Bless us, O Lord, that our sins be forgiven.**

Minister: We pray, O Christ, as the scripture says, "Forgive and you will be forgiven; give and it will be given to you, a good measure, pressed down, shaken together, running over, will be put into your lap; for the measure you give will be the measure you get back." (Luke 8:37-38)

People: **Bless me, O Lord, that I may bless others, through you.**

All: **Amen.**

Silent Prayer

Benediction
Minister: To him who loves us and freed us from our sins with his life's blood, who made of us a royal house, to serve as the priests of his God and Father — to him be glory and dominion for ever and ever!

People: Amen.

(Congregation seated for meditation and adoration.)

The Second Word From The Cross
12:40 P.M.

Hymn "There Is A Green Hill Far Away"

There is a green hill far away,
Outside a city wall,
Where the dear Lord was crucified,
Who died to save us all.

We may not know, we cannot tell,
What pains he had to bear,
But we believe it was for us
He hung and suffered there.

He died that we might be forgiv'n;
He died to make us good,
That we might go at last to heav'n,
Saved by his precious blood.
                    (Cecil Frances Alexander, 1829-1895)

Psalm 31:1-14
Minister: In you, O Lord, I seek refuge;
        do not let me ever be put to shame;
        in your righteousness deliver me.

People: **Incline your ear to me;
  rescue me speedily.
Be a rock of refuge for me,
  a strong fortress to save me.**

Minister: You are indeed my rock and my fortress;
  for your name's sake lead me
    and guide me,

People: **Take me out of the net that is hidden for me,
  for you are my refuge.**

Minister: Into your hand I commit my spirit;
  you have redeemed me, O Lord, faithful God.

People: **You hate those who pay regard
  to worthless idols,
  but I trust in the Lord.**

Minister: I will exult and rejoice in your
    steadfast love,
  because you have seen my affliction;
    you have taken heed of my adversities.

People: **And have not delivered me into the
  hand of the enemy; you have set my
    feet in a broad place.**

Minister: Be gracious to me, O Lord, for I am in distress;
  my eye wastes away from grief, my soul and body
    also.

People: **For my life is spent with sorrow, and my
  years with sighing; my strength fails because
  of my misery, and my bones waste away.**

Minister: I am the scorn of all my adversaries,
a horror to my neighbors, an object of dread to my acquaintances; those who see me in the street flee from me.

People: I have passed out of mind like one who is dead; I have become like a broken vessel.

Minister: For I hear the whispering of many — terror all around! — as they scheme together against me, as they plot to take my life.

People: But I trust in you, O Lord; I say, "You are my God."

The Lesson   Luke 23:35-43

Minister: *And the people stood by, watching; but the leaders scoffed at him, saying, "He saved others; let him save himself if he is the Messiah of God, his chosen one!" The soldiers also mocked him, coming up and offering him sour wine, and saying, "If you are the King of the Jews, save yourself!" There was also an inscription over him, "This is the King of the Jews."*

One of the criminals who were hanged there kept deriding him and saying, "Are you not the Messiah? Save yourself and us!" But the other rebuked him, saying, "Do you not fear God, since you are under the same sentence of condemnation? And we indeed have been condemned justly, for we are getting what we deserve for our deeds, but this man has done nothing wrong." Then he said, "Jesus, remember me when you come into your kingdom." He replied, "Truly I tell you, today you will be with me in Paradise."

Meditation on the Second Word from the Cross

"Truly I tell you, today you will be with me in Paradise." — Luke 23:43

Today is now the hour given,
This is the moment of eternal heaven.
God in Christ is ever here
And so his presence everywhere.

Those three men on the crosses hung;
The thief's angry words at Christ were flung
From one side, "Save thyself and us."
But his companion raised a fuss.

He who answered turned his heavy head,
Rebuking him who hard words said,
"His condemnation is as it should be,
Wrongs from which he cannot flee.

"You only need to look at him,
And see his life is spiritually trim.
I know he's done nothing wrong,
To him, yes, him I would belong.

"Remember me, O Master true.
Change my life; take me with you.
I feel so safe e'en though in this place
I can't view your holy face.

"Though on this hill my cross is trouble,
Here, with you, my blessing twice double,
The nearness of Jesus the Christ,
Make even the last, come first."

"... *today you will be with me in Paradise."*

(WDM)

Hymn   "Jesus, In Thy Dying Woes" Part II
Jesus, pitying the sighs
Of the thief, who near thee dies,
Promising him paradise:
Hear us, holy Jesus.

May we in our guilt and shame
Still thy love and mercy claim,
Calling humbly on thy name:
Hear us, holy Jesus.

May our hearts to thee incline,
Looking from our cross to thine.
Cheer our souls with hope divine:
Hear us, holy Jesus.

(Thomas Benson Pollock, 1836-1896)

Prayer

Minister: O God our Father, who gave to us your only Son, give to us the strength and will to study and understand his word.

People: **Father, hear our prayer.**

Minister: Father, may we follow the example of this thief, who shared a cross next to our Lord. Let faith, as the thief's faith, grow each minute, each hour, each month, each year, as we feel his spirit speaking to and through us, in our struggles of life.

People: **Father, hear our prayer.**

Minister: O Lord, as the great astronomer Copernicus composed a verse to be the epitaph on his tomb, we add these words to our prayer:
> "I ask not such favor as Saint Paul obtained,
> But what, on the cross to the thief thou didst give,
> O Jesus, I fervently pray, grant to me."[1]

People: **Yes, Father, hear this our fervent prayer.**

Minister: Let the world, O Christ, hear this prayer and lift it high to thee!

People: Hear our pleading prayer. Amen.

Silent Prayer

Benediction
Minister: "Grace be with you all who have an undying love for Jesus Christ." (Ephesians 6:24)

People: Amen.

(Congregation seated for meditation and adoration.)

The Third Word From The Cross
1:00 P.M.

Hymn   "Rock Of Ages, Cleft For Me"
Rock of Ages, cleft for me,
Let me hide myself in thee;
Let the water and the blood,
From thy riven side which flowed,
Be of sin the double cure:
Cleanse me from its guilt and pow'r.

Not the labors of my hands
Can fulfill thy law's demands;
Could my zeal no respite know,
Could my tears forever flow,
All for sin could not atone;
Thou must save, and thou alone.

Nothing in my hand I bring;
Simply to thy cross I cling,
Naked, come to thee for dress;
Helpless, look to thee for grace;
Foul, I to the fountain fly;
Wash me, Savior, or I die.

While I draw this fleeting breath,
When mine eyelids close in death,
When I soar to worlds unknown,
See thee on thy judgment throne,
Rock of Ages, cleft for me,
Let me hide myself in thee.

                      (Augustus Montague Toplady, 1740-1778)

Psalm 38

Minister: O Lord, do not rebuke me in your anger,
or discipline me in your wrath.

People: **For your arrows have sunk into me,
and your hand has come down on me.**

Minister: There is no soundness in my flesh
because of your indignation;
there is no health in my bones
because of my sin.

People: **For my iniquities have gone over my head;
they weigh like a burden too heavy for me.**

Minister: My wounds grow foul and fester because of
my foolishness;

People: **I am utterly bowed down and prostrate;
all day long I go around mourning.**

Minister: For my loins are filled with burning,
and there is no soundness in my flesh.

People: **I am utterly spent and crushed;
I groan because of the tumult of my heart.**

Minister: O Lord, all my longing is known to you;
my sighing is not hidden from you.

People: My heart throbs, my strength fails me;
    as for the light of my eyes — it
    also has gone from me.

Minister: My friends and companions stand aloof
    from my affliction,
    and my neighbors stand far off.

People: Those who seek my life lay their snares;
    those who seek to hurt me speak of ruin,
    and meditate treachery all day long.

Minister: But I am like the deaf, I do not hear;
    like the mute, who cannot speak.

People: Truly, I am like one who does not hear,
    and in whose mouth is no retort.

Minister: But it is for you, O Lord, that I wait;
    it is you, O Lord my God, who will
    answer.

People: For I pray, "Only do not let them rejoice
    over me, those who boast against me when
    my foot slips."

Minister: For I am ready to fall,
    and my pain is ever with me.

People: I confess my iniquity;
    I am sorry for my sin.

Minister: Those who are my foes without cause are mighty,
    and many are those who hate me wrongfully.

People: Those who render me evil for good are my
    adversaries because I follow after good.

Minister: Do not forsake me, O Lord;
O my God, do not be far from me;

People: **Make haste to help me,
O Lord, my salvation.**

The Lesson John 19:23-27
Minister: *When the soldiers had crucified Jesus, they took his clothes and divided them into four parts, one for each soldier. They also took his tunic; now the tunic was seamless, woven in one piece from the top, so they said to one another, "Let us not tear it, but cast lots for it to see who will get it." This was to fulfill what the scripture says.*

"They divided my clothes among themselves,
and for my clothing they cast lots."

And that is what the soldiers did. Meanwhile, standing near the cross of Jesus were his mother, and his mother's sister, Mary the wife of Clopas, and Mary Magdalene. When Jesus saw his mother and the disciple whom he loved standing beside her, he said to his mother, "Woman, here is your son." Then he said to the disciple, "Here is your mother." And from that hour the disciple took her into his own home.

Meditation on the Third Word from the Cross
"When Jesus saw his mother and the disciple whom he loved standing beside her, he said to his mother, 'Woman, here is your son.' Then he said to the disciple, 'Here is your mother.'" — John 19:26-27

John and Mary, side by side,
His mother and loved disciple closely tied
Courageous, to stand at the cross close by
Under that dark and foreboding sky.

Her heart, love filled, from the babe's first cry,
And John, beloved in the Master's eye,
This follower known as "Thunder's son,"
She and her son always one.

John, you recall, with brother James,
Sought high position, political fame.
But Christ was quick to speak his will
And say, high positions he did not fill.

Friends, so close, John and The One,
His service in Christ had just begun.
The Holy Spirit's presence would soon descend,
And John's gifts of service would be without end.

His great pen gave "Three-sixteen,"
Luke though Mary would pen supreme,
The high priestly prayer Saint John had done,
In Mary's heart, her hurt just begun.

Christ though dying on the cross so near
His words came forth for all to hear:
"Woman, here is your son."
Then to the disciple, *"Here is your mother."*

(WDM)

Hymn "Jesus, In Thy Dying Woes" Part III
Jesus, loving to the end
Her whose heart thy sorrows rend,
And thy dearest human friend:
Hear us, holy Jesus.

May we in thy sorrows share,
For thy sake all peril dare,
And enjoy thy tender care:
Hear us, holy Jesus.

May we all thy loved ones be,
All one holy family,
Loving for the love of thee:
Hear us, holy Jesus.

(Thomas Benson Pollock, 1836-1896)

The Prayer

Minister: Let us pray. O Christ, as you always set for us an example through your own prayer life, help us, as followers, to follow this path in our praying.

People: **Yes, O Christ, let us lead our families in our own personal life of prayer.**

Minister: As you, O Lord, showed constant, loving respect for your family, especially your mother, lead us to do the same in our homes.

People: **We implore you, O Father, that we may be as loving and considerate to our families, husbands and wives, mothers and fathers, sisters and brothers, our neighbors and people of the world, as you have requested us to be.**

Minister: We would pray in the spirit, with which Paul wrote to his dear friend Timothy, "I am reminded of your sincere faith, a faith that lived first in your grandmother Lois and your mother Eunice, and now, I am sure, lives in you. For this reason, I remind you to rekindle the gift of God that is within you."

People: **O yes, Christ, let the fire of your spirit burn within our hearts and our homes and our lives, that we may always follow your lead.**

Minister: O God, we pray for ourselves and all persons, whatever the situations of our lives may be. Take away our pride and selfishness, and let us be allowed to see the precious worth of those around us. Let us see and respect the many "above" and "below" us in age, intellect, personality, and position: through your Son, Jesus Christ our Lord and Savior.

People: **Help us all, we pray, O Lord.**

Minister: And now, to him who loves us and freed us from our sins with his life's blood, to him be glory and dominion for ever and ever.

People: **Amen.**

(Congregation seated for meditation and adoration.)

The Fourth Word From The Cross
1:25 P.M.

Hymn "Alas! And Did My Savior Bleed"

Alas! And did my Savior bleed,
And did my sov'reign die?
Would he devote that sacred head
For sinners such as I?

Was it for sins that I had done
He groaned upon the tree?
Amazing pity, grace unknown,
And love beyond degree!

Well might the sun in darkness hide
And shut its glories in
When God, the mighty maker, died
For his own creatures' sin.

Thus might I hide my blushing face
While his dear cross appears,
Dissolve my heart in thankfulness,
And melt my eyes to tears.

But tears of grief cannot repay
The debt of love I owe;
Here, Lord, I give myself away:
It's all that I can do.

(Isaac Watts, 1674-1748)

Psalm 22

Minister: My God, my God, why have you forsaken me?
Why are you so far from helping me,
from the words of my groaning?

People: **O my God, I cry by day, but you do not answer;
and by night, but find no rest.**

Minister: Yet you are holy, enthroned on the
praises of Israel.

People: **In you our ancestors trusted;
they trusted, and you delivered them.**

Minister: To you they cried, and were saved;
in you they trusted, and were not put to shame.

People: **But I am a worm, and not human;
scorned by others, and despised by the people.**

Minister: All who see me mock at me; they make
mouths at me, they shake their heads;

People: **"Commit your cause to the Lord; let him deliver —
let him rescue the one in whom he delights!"**

Minister: Yet it was you who took me from the womb;
   you kept me safe on my mother's breast.

People: **On you I was cast from my birth,
   and since my mother bore me
   you have been my God.**

Minister: Do not be far from me, for trouble is near
   and there is no help.

People: **Many bulls encircle me, strong bulls
   of Bashan surround me;**

Minister: They open wide their mouths at me,
   like a ravening and roaring lion.

People: **I am poured out like water, and all
   my bones are out of joint;
   my heart is like wax;
   it is melted within my breast;**

Minister: My mouth is dried up like a potsherd,
   and my tongue sticks to my jaws;
   you lay me in the dust of death.

   For dogs are all around me;
   a company of evildoers encircles me.
   My hands and feet have shriveled;

People: **I can count all my bones.
   They stare and gloat over me;**

Minister: They divide my clothes among themselves,
   and for my clothing they cast lots.

People: **But you, O Lord, do not be far away!
   O my help, come quickly to my aid!**

Minister: Deliver my soul from the sword,
my life from the power of the dog!

People: **Save me from the mouth of the lion!
From the horns of the wild oxen
you have rescued me.**

Minister: I will tell of your name to my
brothers and sisters; in the midst of the
congregation I will praise you:

People: **You who fear the Lord, praise him!
All you offspring of Jacob, glorify him;
stand in awe of him, all you
offspring of Israel!**

Minister: For he did not despise or abhor
the affliction of the afflicted;
he did not hide his face from me,
but heard when I cried to him.

People: **From you comes my praise in the great
congregation; my vows I will pay
before those who fear him.**

Minister: The poor shall eat and be satisfied;
those who seek him shall praise
the Lord.
May your hearts live forever!

People: **All the ends of the earth shall
remember and turn to the Lord;
and all the families of the
nations shall worship before him.**

Minister: For dominion belongs to the Lord,
and he rules over the nations.

People: To him, indeed, shall all who sleep in the earth bow down; before him shall bow all who go down to the dust, and I shall live for him.

Minister: Posterity will serve him; future generations will be told about the Lord,

People: And proclaim his deliverance to a people yet unborn, saying that he has done it.

Minister: Glory be to the Father, and to the Son, and to the Holy Spirit. As it was in the beginning, is now, and will be forever.

People: Amen.

The Lesson   Matthew 27:45-49

Minister: *From noon on, darkness came over the whole land until three in the afternoon. And about three o'clock, Jesus cried with a loud voice, "E'li, E'li, le-ma' sa-bach'tha-ni?" that is, "My God, my God, why have you forsaken me?" When some of the bystanders heard it, they said, "This man is calling for Elijah." At once one of them ran and got a sponge, filled it with sour wine, put it on a stick, and gave it to him to drink. But the others said, "Wait, let us see whether Elijah will come to save him."*

Meditation on the Fourth Word from the Cross
"My God, my God, why have you forsaken me?" — Matthew 27:46

"My God, my God ..." don't abandon me;
Here words of past loneliness to see.
Words through struggle of sinful man,
The heavy weights on Christ descend.

The pain so sharp, a hideous wrong,
The struggle of Christ, he suffered long

Even the sins that we, yes, we, commit
Upon this man, our God, they never fit.

How large this clumsy, human load!
To run away? No bypass road,
He hung right there on Calvary.
He cried out from his, our, human misery.

I feel, don't you, the horrible weight
My intended good, so very often late,
But through his help, and suffering so
A better path of life I, we, know.

We often echo, "God, don't abandon me."
I now know you really do see
You'll never, no, never let me fall,
Now and for all time, I hear your call.

"My God, my God, why have you forsaken me?"

(WDM)

Hymn "Jesus, In Thy Dying Woes" Part IV
Jesus, whelmed in fears unknown,
With our evil left alone,
While no light from heav'n is shown:
Hear us, holy Jesus.

When we seem in vain to pray
And our hope seems far away,
In the darkness be our stay:
Hear us, holy Jesus.

Though no Father seem to hear,
Though no light our spirits cheer,
May we know that God is near:
Hear us, holy Jesus.

(Thomas Benson Pollock, 1836-1896)

The Prayer
Minister: Let us pray. Father, we come to you in our full humanity, on this very special day of memorial to you and special time of remembrance in our lives. Our human frailties we feel so strong and confess to you in our time of need.

People: **We confess to you, O Lord.**

Minister: O Father, you know the weakness of our lives. We plead for your forgiveness. Give us love and your constant care and your strength.

People: **We confess to you, O Lord.**

Minister: We come to you in prayer as your children. Please, O Lord, let your spirit fill our lives and our actions as we come to know your will for each of us.

People: **Hear our prayer, O Lord.**

Minister: Turn not away from us and do not forsake us in these days of our struggles. O Lord, let your hand lift us, let your hand guide us, let your hand comfort us every minute, of every hour, of every day.

People: **Hear our prayer, O Christ.**

All: **Amen.**

Benediction
Minister: Guard what has been trusted to us, our faith, our hope, and our love; through Christ our Lord.

People: **Amen.**

(Congregation seated for meditation and adoration.)

The Fifth Word From The Cross
1:45 P.M.

Hymn   "Ah, Holy Jesus"

Ah, holy Jesus, how hast thou offended
That man to judge thee hath in hate pretended?
By foes derided, by thine own rejected,
   O most afflicted.

Who was the guilty? Who brought this upon thee?
Alas, my treason, Jesus, hath undone thee.
'Twas I, Lord Jesus, I it was denied thee;
   I crucified thee.

Lo, the Good Shepherd for the sheep is offered;
The slave hath sinned, and the Son hath suffered;
For man's atonement, while he nothing heedeth,
   God intercedeth.

For me, kind Jesus, was thine incarnation,
Thy mortal sorrow, and thy life's oblation;
Thy death of anguish and thy bitter Passion,
   For my salvation.

Therefore, kind Jesus, since I cannot pay thee,
I do adore thee, and will ever pray thee;
Think on thy pity and thy love unswerving,
   Not my deserving.

                              (Johann Heermann, 1585-1647;
                               tr. Robert Bridges, 1844-1930)

Psalm 102
Minister: Hear my prayer, O Lord;
               let my cry come to you.

People: Do not hide your face from me
               in the day of my distress.

>   Incline your ear to me; answer
>   me speedily in the day when I call.

Minister: For my days pass away like smoke,
>   and my bones burn like a furnace.

People: My heart is stricken and withered like grass;
>   I am too wasted to eat my bread.

Minister: Because of my loud groaning
>   my bones cling to my skin.

People: I am like an owl of the wilderness,
>   like a little owl of the waste places.

Minister: I lie awake;
>   I am like a lonely bird on the housetop.

People: All day long my enemies taunt me;
>   those who deride me use my name for a curse.

Minister: For I eat ashes like bread,
>   and mingle tears with my drink,

People: Because of your indignation and anger;
>   for you have lifted me up and thrown me aside.

Minister: My days are like an evening shadow;
>   I wither away like grass.

People: But you, O Lord, are enthroned forever;
>   your name endures to all generations.

Minister: You will rise up and have compassion on Zion,
>   for it is time to favor it;
>   the appointed time has come.

People: For your servants hold its stones dear,
and have pity on its dust.

Minister: The nations will fear the name of the Lord,
and all the kings of the earth your glory.

People: For the Lord will build up Zion;
he will appear in his glory.

Minister: He will regard the prayer of the destitute,
and will not despise their prayer.

People: Let this be recorded for a generation to come,
so that a people yet unborn may
praise the Lord:

Minister: That he looked down from his holy height,
from heaven the Lord looked at the earth,

People: To hear the groans of the prisoners,
to set free those who were doomed to die;

Minister: So that the name of the Lord
may be declared in Zion, and his praise
in Jerusalem,

People: When peoples gather together, and kingdoms,
to worship the Lord.

Minister: He has broken my strength in mid-course;
he has shortened my days.

People: "O my God," I say, "do not take me away
at the midpoint of my life, you whose
years endure throughout all generations."

Minister: Long ago you laid the foundation of the earth,
and the heavens are the work of your hands.

People: **They will perish, but you endure;
they will all wear out like a garment.
You change them like clothing, and they pass away;**

Minister: But you are the same, and your years have no end.

People: **The children of your servants shall live secure;
their offspring shall be established in
your presence.**

All: **Glory be to the Father, and to the Son, and to the Holy Spirit, as it was in the beginning, is now and ever shall be, world without end. Amen.**

The Lesson   John 19:28-29
Minister: *After this, when Jesus knew that all was now finished, he said (in order to fulfill the scripture), "I am thirsty." A jar full of sour wine was standing there. So they put a sponge full of the wine on a branch of hyssop and held it to his mouth.*

Meditation on the Fifth Word from the Cross
"... I am thirsty." — John 19:28b

Sometimes with joy we nearly burst,
Sometimes it's tears we long have nursed,
But now his task is nearly over.
His physical needs, the last he covered.

He thinks of others time after time,
To think of self first, never was prime.
That's why he came to fill our thirst,
And give our lives best things first.

He seeks for self after others are sought.
With the selfish life only trouble is bought.
Out of his abundant love it's clear,
He thought of others, to him so dear.

Now that his task was nearly done,
All calls answered, every race run,
Christ's dry, parched throat nearly burst,
And cried out strongly, humanly, "I thirst."
Yes, he called!

"I am thirsty."

(WDM)

Hymn "Jesus, In Thy Dying Woes" Part V
Jesus, in thy thirst and pain,
While thy wounds thy lifeblood drain,
Thirsting more our love to gain:
   Hear us, holy Jesus.

Thirst for us in mercy still;
All thy holy work fulfill;
Satisfy thy loving will:
   Hear us, holy Jesus.

May we thirst thy love to know;
Lead us in our sin and woe
Where the healing waters flow:
   Hear us, Holy Jesus.

(Thomas Benson Pollock, 1836-1896)

Prayer
Minister: Our Father God, you who did give us your own son through the womb of a woman, and thus did give your son human form, just as ours: we thank you for such a gift, as our own, God in human form. Yes, we now hear his human needs and pains as he thirsts for water.

People: O Christ, we hear your cry of human pain, and we know through you the weight of our sin, which you carry upon the cross. It's this pain our sins have brought. Forgive us, O Christ!

Minister: Your Son, our Savior, as he lived and walked with his disciples, did pluck the grain and eat on the Sabbath. Let us follow in his steps and his example to form our way of life.

People: Let us, O Christ, study and know the Word you gave to us — the Word you are and the words of scripture — that the pattern of your life be the manner of our daily living. As you guide, may we follow, day by day.

Minister: Let not food, drink, clothing, and all material things be our goal and desire of life; but let the spiritual goals take the primary place in our lives. Thus we shall worship our Lord first in a love like your love, and love our neighbor as ourselves.

People: Hear our prayer, O Christ.

Minister: Let your church, O Christ, follow the words of one of the youth hymns from the early years of this century:

> Then onward be the war-cry
> And onward still, so long
> As we have self to conquer,
> Souls to cheer with song.
>
> Let sound the martial music,
> Ring out the bugle call
> To rally for the conflict
> Our people one and all.

> We proudly bear as banner
> A cross within the heart,
> To show that we have chosen
> Christ, the better part ...
>
> All hail, our glorious Savior!
> We march where thou hast trod,
> To seek thy house of triumph,
> The city of our God.
>
> (Lillian Weaver Cassady, 1893;
> Refrain: Margaret Seebach, 1915)

People: **Hear this, our prayer, O Christ.**

Minister: Our heavenly Father, we seek help for all men, women, and children upon whom many crosses have been laid; nations which are plagued with famine, sickness, war; for Christians who are suffering because of their faith; for persons on sea, land, or in the air; for anyone oppressed with poverty, sickness, distress of body, mind, our soul.

People: **We thirst in many ways, O God; satisfy our thirst.**

Minister: O Lord, as we recall your physical pain and distress, your completed bodily sacrifice for each of us, may we now accept the peace which you have given to us. Let us relive the meaning of the cross, and live in brotherhood and love with each other until we have obeyed your will for our lives.

People: **Amen. Come, Lord Jesus.**

Minister: The grace of our Lord Jesus Christ be with all the saints. Amen.

(Congregation seated for meditation and adoration.)

The Sixth Word From The Cross
2:15 P.M.

Hymn "O Sacred Head, Now Wounded"

O sacred head, now wounded,
With grief and shame weighed down,
Now scornfully surrounded
With thorns, thine only crown;
O sacred head, what glory,
What bliss till now was thine!
Yet, though despised and gory,
I joy to call thee mine.

How art thou pale with anguish,
With sore abuse and scorn;
How does that visage languish
Which once was bright as morn!
Thy grief and bitter Passion
Were all for sinners' gain;
Mine, mine was the transgression,
But thine the deadly pain.

What language shall I borrow
To thank thee, dearest friend,
For this thy dying sorrow,
Thy pity without end?
Oh, make me thine forever,
And should I fainting be,
Lord, let me never, never
Outlive my love to thee.

Lord, be my consolation;
Shield me when I must die;
Remind me of thy Passion
When my last hour draws nigh.
These eyes, new faith receiving,
From thee shall never move;

For he who dies believing
Dies safely in thy love.
> (Attr. Bernard of Clairvaux, 1091-1153;
> tr. Paul Gerhardt, 1607-1676)

Psalm 130
Minister: Out of the depths I cry to you, O Lord.

People: **Lord, hear my voice! Let your ears be attentive to the voice of my supplications!**

Minister: If you, O Lord, should mark iniquities, Lord, who could stand?

People: **But there is forgiveness with you, so that you may be revered.**

Minister: I wait for the Lord, my soul waits, and in his word I hope;

People: **My soul waits for the Lord more than those who watch for the morning, more than those who watch for the morning.**

Minister: O Israel, hope in the Lord! For with the Lord there is steadfast love, and with him is great power to redeem.

People: **It is he who will redeem Israel from all its iniquities.**

The Lesson John 19:30
Minister: *When Jesus had received the wine, he said, "It is finished." Then he bowed his head and gave up his spirit.*

Meditation on the Sixth Word from the Cross
"It is finished." — John 19:30a

This is it, his eternal plan,
His intention overflowing from his Father's hand.
All that he had hoped, from Mary's pure womb,
Now on our horizon did clearly loom.

A sign of completion by Christ is given
For every last soul, born under heaven.
He loved all and gave to their need
Heaven bound! They, too, by his holy deed.

All completed to his satisfaction
Birth made known through angelic action,
The news shepherds told in Bethlehem town
Now spreads to all the world around.

He often would pause, take a long, long look,
Knowing his guide was God's Holy Book.
The old had Good News from long ago,
The new, now redemption was ready to show.

He looked beyond the cross to dark, dark clouds,
Opened his mouth, his soul, and spoke aloud,
"I like what I see, lives redeemed, replenished,"
With clearness of voice Jesus said, *"It is finished."*

(WDM)

Prayer

Minister: Let us pray. Jesus said to them, "My food is to do the will of him who sent me and to complete his work." Let us, O Christ, take up the work he is giving us to do and follow his lead now, today.

People: **Let us listen, O Christ, and follow his lead.**

Minister: Dear Lord Christ, as you have said, "I came from the Father and have come into the world; again, I am leaving the world and going to the Father." The disciples said, "Yes, now you are speaking plainly, not in any figure of speech; now we know that you know all things, and do not need to have anyone question you; by this we believe that you came from God."

People: **O Lord, continue to strengthen our faith, we pray.**

Minister: Now, O Christ, we hear again your words from the cross: that your work is coming to an end. At this time, we recall the prayer that John wrote in his Gospel account: "Father, glorify your Son so that your Son may glorify you. You have given him authority over all people, to give eternal life to all whom you have given him, and this is eternal life, that they may know you, the only true God, and Jesus Christ, whom you have sent. I glorify you on earth by finishing the work that you gave me to do...." Hear our prayer.

People: **Let us, O Christ, your believing, faithful followers, follow your lead that your apostles and disciples have given and still give to us through the holy scriptures. Hear these, we plead, our fervent prayers.**

All: **Amen. Come, Lord Jesus.**

Hymn "Jesus, In Thy Dying Woes" Part VI

Jesus, all our ransom paid,
All thy Father's will obeyed;
By thy suff'rings perfect made:
Hear us, holy Jesus.

Save us in our soul's distress;
Be our help to cheer and bless,
While we grow in holiness:
Hear us, holy Jesus.

Brighten all our heav'nward way
With an ever holier ray
Till we pass to perfect day:
Hear us, holy Jesus.

                    (Thomas Benson Pollock, 1836-1896)

Minister: To him who loves us and freed us from our sins with his life's blood, who made of us a royal house, to serve as the priests of his God and Father — to him be glory and dominion for ever and ever!

People: **Amen.**

(Congregation seated for meditation and adoration.)

The Seventh Word From The Cross
2:35 P.M.

Hymn   "Were You There When They Crucified My Lord?"
Were you there when they crucified my Lord?
Were you there when they crucified my Lord?
Oh, sometimes it causes me to tremble, tremble, tremble.
Were you there when they crucified my Lord?

Were you there when they nailed him to the tree?
Were you there when they nailed him to the tree?
Oh, sometimes it causes me to tremble, tremble, tremble.
Were you there when they nailed him to the tree?

Were you there when they took him from the tree?
Were you there when they took him from the tree?
Oh, sometimes it causes me to tremble, tremble, tremble.
Were you there when they took him from the tree?*

Were you there when they laid him in the tomb?
Were you there when they laid him in the tomb?

Oh, sometimes it causes me to tremble, tremble, tremble.
Were you there when they laid him in the tomb?

(Winfred Douglas, 1867-1944)

(*Added for this service only.)

Psalm 31:1-5, 14-17, 19-24

Minister: In you, O Lord, I seek refuge; do not let me ever be put to shame; in your righteousness deliver me.

People: **Incline your ear to me; rescue me speedily. Be a rock of refuge for me, a strong fortress to save me.**

Minister: You are indeed my rock and my fortress; for your name's sake lead me and guide me,

People: **Take me out of the net that is hidden for me, for you are my refuge.**

Minister: Into your hand I commit my spirit; you have redeemed me, O Lord, faithful God.

People: **But I trust in you, O Lord; I say, "You are my God."**

Minister: My times are in your hand; deliver me from the hand of my enemies and persecutors.

People: **Let your face shine upon your servant; save me in your steadfast love.**

Minister: Do not let me be put to shame, O Lord, for I call on you; let the wicked be put to shame; let them go dumbfounded to Sheol.

People: **O how abundant is your goodness that you have laid up for those who fear you, and accomplished for those who take refuge in you, in the sight of everyone!**

Minister: In the shelter of your presence you made them from human plots; you hold them safe under your shelter from contentious tongues.

People: **Blessed be the Lord, for he has wondrously shown his steadfast love to me when I was beset as a city under siege.**

Minister: I had said in my alarm, "I am driven far from your sight." But you heard my supplications when I cried out to you for help.

People: **Love the Lord, all you his saints. The Lord preserves the faithful, but abundantly repays the one who acts haughtily.**

Minister: Be strong and let your heart take courage, all you who wait for the Lord.

In the name of the Father, and of the Son, and of the Holy Spirit.

All: **Amen.**

The Lesson   Luke 23:44-49
Minister: *It was now about noon, and darkness came over the whole land until three in the afternoon, while the sun's light failed; and the curtain of the temple was torn in two. Then Jesus, crying with a loud voice, said, "Father, into your hands I commend my Spirit." And having said this, he breathed his last.* (Pause for a moment of silence.) *When the centurion saw what had taken place, he praised God and said, "Certainly this man was innocent." And when all the crowds who had gathered there for this spectacle saw what had taken place, they returned home, beating their breasts. But all his acquaintances, including the women who had followed*

him from Galilee, stood at a distance, watching these things.

Meditation on the Seventh Word from the Cross
Minister: "Grace be to you, and peace from God our Father and our Jesus Christ."

"Father, into your hands I commend my spirit." — Luke 23:46a

Is it over, or just begun?
The hope, is it gone, as the set of the sun?
Love, did it vanish, and fade away
Never to be felt again in our day?

Is it over, or just begun?
He said, "The Father and I are one."
He called the disciples, and taught them true.
The souls he wanted to be all new.

The question sings out, crisp and clear,
Did we lose our Christ, so very dear?
The soldier at the cross gave his nod,
I believe "... this was the Son of God."

His spirit in me?
Yes, that's where it can be;
Christ breathes in us God's Deity.
That's God in us, his perfect reality.

Now view his body
With spear and nail made bloody.
The viewers thought, this is the end.
But now, his life will surely mend.

Jesus to this crowd seemed very pathetic.
They didn't know he is fully prophetic,

And in order to end our forlorn strife
He gave continuous, unending, glorious life.

His Godly light seemed to grow dim;
Disciples will soon tell the truth about him.
Love does not vanish, that dread cross day,
Eternal blessings for the world, they'll stay!

No! No! It's not over; it's just begun!
The Good News, the Gospel, spreads like the light of the sun!

"Father, into your hands, I commend my spirit!"

(WDM)

Hymn "Jesus, In Thy Dying Woes" Part VII
Jesus, all thy labor vast,
All thy woe and conflict past;
Yielding up thy soul at last:
    Hear us, holy Jesus.

When the death shades round us low'r,
Guard us from the tempter's pow'r.
Keep us in that trial hour:
    Hear us, holy Jesus.

May thy life and death supply
Grace to live and grace to die,
Grace to reach the home on high:
    Hear us, holy Jesus.

(Thomas Benson Pollock, 1836-1896)

Prayer
Minister: Let us pray. O Christ, now as we near the close of this hour of worship, we recall the words that you gave through John's Gospel, that you, when you were lifted up, would draw all people to you. Our Lord, we pray with fervent plea that each of us will be included in that

great body of believing followers of your congregations throughout this world.

People: **Hear our prayer, O Christ.**

Minister: Dear Lord, we now echo the thoughts of your apostle, the fervent missionary Paul, that we too glory in your cross, knowing now that it is through the cross that all of us in this world may be saved.

People: **Father, we pray this in the name of your Son, our Lord and our Savior, Jesus, the Christ.**

Minister: Let us be able to wait for you with a patience like yours, for you are nearer to us than our very breath. You know through your own painful cross experience, our experience of such things as burdens, sorrow, paths of danger, physical disasters, and illness. Help us in all such things.

People: **Father, into your hands we do place our spirits.**

Minister: O Lord, open all the hearts of the people who hunger and thirst for peace through you, the Christ of the whole world. Let the day arrive when all persons shall discover the great joy and salvation in Jesus Christ our almighty and saving Lord and God.

People: **Amen. Come, Lord Jesus!**

All: **Worthy is the lamb, the lamb that was slain, to receive all power and wealth, wisdom and might, honor and glory and praise!**

Praise and honor, glory and might, to him who sits on the throne and to the lamb forever and ever. Great

and marvelous are thy deeds, O Lord God, sovereign over all; just and true are thy ways, thou king of the ages. Who shall not revere thee, Lord, and do homage to thy name? For thou alone art holy.

All nations shall come and worship in thy presence. For thy just dealings stand revealed. Alleluia! The Lord our God, sovereign over all, has entered his reign!

Minister: May the God of peace, who brought up from the dead our Lord Jesus, the Great Shepherd of the sheep, by the blood of the eternal covenant, make you perfect in all goodness so that you may do his will; and may he make of us what he would have us to be through Jesus Christ, to whom be glory for ever and ever!

All: Amen.

Hymn "Glory Be To Jesus"
Glory be to Jesus, who, in bitter pains,
Poured for me the lifeblood from his sacred veins!

Grace and life eternal in that blood I find;
Blest be his compassion, infinitely kind.

Blest through endless ages be the precious stream
Which from endless torment did the world redeem.

Abel's blood for vengeance pleaded to the skies;
But the blood of Jesus for our pardon cries.

Oft as earth exulting wafts its praise on high,
Angel-hosts, rejoicing, make their glad reply.

Lift we then our voices, swell the mighty flood;
Louder still and louder praise the precious blood!

Amen.

(Italian 18th Century;
Trans. Edward Caswell, 1814-1878)

(When the ministers have left the front of the church, the people may kneel, silently pray, and then leave the church reverently without speaking.)

---

1. *Sermons and Outlines of the Seven Words*, W. W. Robertson and others, p. 37.

I am most indebted to Ms. Gert Fisher, who assisted me in typing this manuscript. Ms. Fisher is a member of St. John's Lutheran Church, Cherryville, North Carolina.

www.ingramcontent.com/pod-product-compliance
Lightning Source LLC
Chambersburg PA
CBHW071800040426
42446CB00012B/2642